Bugs, Bugs, Bugs!

Mary Reid • Betsey Chessen

Scholastic Inc.

New York • Toronto • London • Auckland • Sydney

Acknowledgments

Science Consultants: Patrick R. Thomas, Ph.D., Bronx Zoo/Wildlife Conservation Park; Glenn Phillips, The New York Botanical Garden; **Literacy Specialist:** Maria Utefsky, Reading Recovery Coordinator, District 2, New York City

Design: MKR Design, Inc.

Photo Research: Barbara Scott

Endnotes: Susan Russell

Photographs: Cover: C.K. Lorenz/Photo Researchers, Inc.; p. 1: Robert & Linda Mitchell; p. 2-3: John Gerlach/DRK Photo; p. 2: (bl) N. Smythe/Photo Researchers, Inc.; p.3: (b) Stanley Breeden/DRK Photo; p. 4-5: Michael Fogden/DRK Photo; p. 4: (bl) D.R. Specker/Animals, Animals; p. 5: (b) Matt Meadows/Peter Arnold, Inc.; p. 6-7: Hans Pfletschinger/Peter Arnold, Inc.; p. 6: (l) C.A. Henley; p. 7: (r) Dwight Kuhn; p. 8-9: Robert & Linda Mitchell; p. 8: (l) Robert & Linda Mitchell; p. 9: (c) Dwight Kuhn/DRK Photo; p. 10: Patti Murray/Animals, Animals; p. 11: Robert & Linda Mitchell; p. 12: C.K. Lorenz/Photo Researchers, Inc.

Library of Congress Cataloging-in-Publication Data
Reid, Mary.
Bugs, bugs, bugs! / Mary Reid, Betsey Chessen.
p. cm. -- (Science emergent readers)
"Scholastic early childhood."--P. [4] of cover.
Includes index.
Summary: Photographs and simple text show some of the diversity found in anatomies of insects.
ISBN 0-590-39792-3 (pbk.: alk.paper)
1. Insects--Anatomy--Juvenile literature. [1. Insects.]
I. Chessen, Betsey, 1970-. II. Title. III. Series.
QL494.R45 1998
595.7--dc21   97-29202
                                                                      CIP AC

9   10   03   02   01   00   99

Bugs, bugs, bugs!

Wings, wings, wings!

Legs, legs, legs!

Eyes, eyes, eyes!

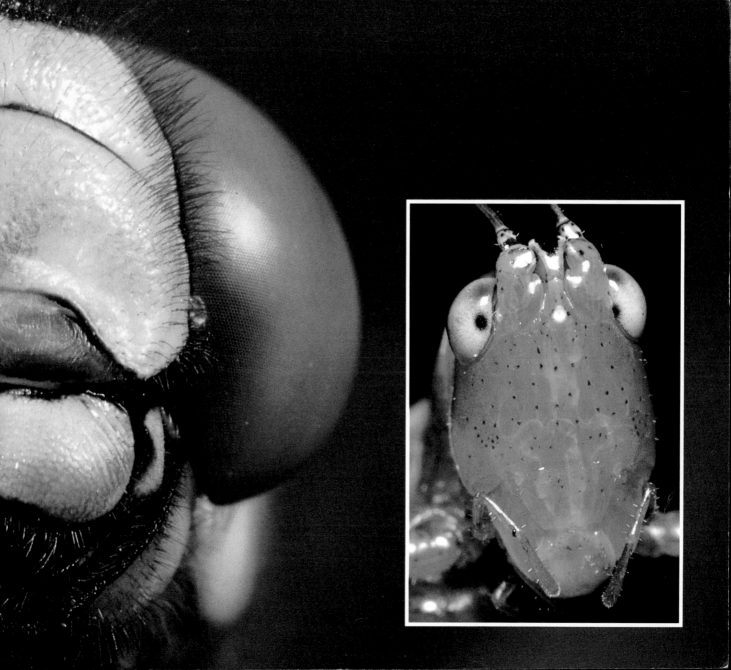

Mouths, mouths, mouths!

Bugs,

bugs,

Bugs, Bugs, Bugs!

"Bug" is the everyday name we use for "insect," and we find bugs everywhere, in all shapes and sizes. Some of the things they have in common are the ability to fly, an external skeleton, adaptability to different foods and conditions, and metamorphosis. The Harvester Ants (left), which collect leftover grain and seeds from fields, are shown swarming at the entrance to their nest.

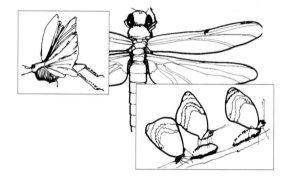

Many insects have wings so they can fly to find food and escape enemies. The grasshopper (left) not only flies but is a champion jumper. The Dewy Dragonfly (center) most closely resembles the insects' prehistoric relatives in that it cannot fold its wings. Butterflies, like the Union Jacks (right), fold their wings and press them together overhead when not in flight.

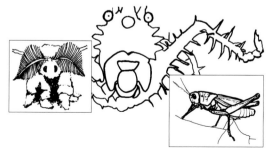

Bug legs come in many different shapes. The Polyphemus Moth (left) has legs that are quite fuzzy, while the Spike-headed Katydid (center) has spike-covered legs. Katydids are usually green and are known for their summer songs. The Eastern Lubber Grasshopper (right) can jump up to 20 times its own length using powerful muscles in its thorax.

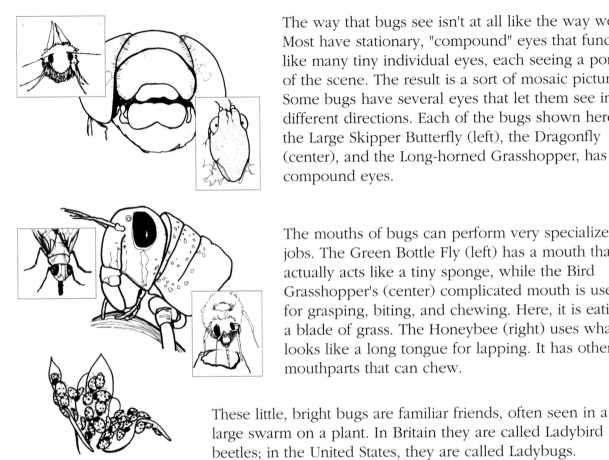

The way that bugs see isn't at all like the way we do. Most have stationary, "compound" eyes that function like many tiny individual eyes, each seeing a portion of the scene. The result is a sort of mosaic picture. Some bugs have several eyes that let them see in different directions. Each of the bugs shown here, the Large Skipper Butterfly (left), the Dragonfly (center), and the Long-horned Grasshopper, has compound eyes.

The mouths of bugs can perform very specialized jobs. The Green Bottle Fly (left) has a mouth that actually acts like a tiny sponge, while the Bird Grasshopper's (center) complicated mouth is used for grasping, biting, and chewing. Here, it is eating a blade of grass. The Honeybee (right) uses what looks like a long tongue for lapping. It has other mouthparts that can chew.

These little, bright bugs are familiar friends, often seen in a large swarm on a plant. In Britain they are called Ladybird beetles; in the United States, they are called Ladybugs.